Leela and
the Days of Rain

RITA PATEL GARCIA, LCSW, RYT

Acknowledgments

Thank you to all who reviewed
the story prior to publication.

Your suggestions and support made this book
possible and Leela's story much better.

Daniel Horowitz Garcia; Maci Daye, LPC, CHT;
Noureen Ahmed, LMSW; Joya Banerjee;
Katie Fahrenbruch; Dr. Connie Holliman, LPC, NCC;
Nita Patel, MPH, DrPH.; Asha Patel, MEd, LMT;
Guneeta Singh, LMSW; Amy Robbins, LPC, RPT;
Alka Roy; Mayuresh Tapale; Jyoti Kaneria;
Anna Montford Shepard, and Carole Moore.

For all those not named, you have my deepest thanks.
I'm grateful for your presence in my life.

Dedication

This book is dedicated to my parents, Nirmala and Ramesh Patel. Their sacrifice and struggle made this book, my career, and my life in this country possible.

Thank you for everything you have done.

Once upon a time, there was
a little-big girl named Leela.
Leela loved many things.
She loved playing with her friends.
She loved nature - the birds,
the butterflies, the rain and the sun.

One day, Leela found out that she and her family had to leave their home. When they left, they were only able to take a few things with them. Leela left behind her friends, her toys, and all her favorite things.

As she climbed the steps at the airport, Leela's happiness began to drift off with the clouds. Gone were the days of rain.

Now in her new home, Leela missed the days of rain. Of rain so soft, it caressed her face. Rain so cool, it made her smile. Rain so powerful, the flowers fell to the ground, kissing the earth. Rain which brought a breath of fresh sweet air to Leela.

Now came days mixed with sadness and stillness. Leela missed home and didn't feel like playing anymore.

Leela's sadness mixed with silence.
Silence grew into fear.
Fear grew bigger
and bigger until
Leela couldn't
breathe. Oh,
how hard it
was for Leela
to breathe!
When she
tried to take
a breath,
the air just
seemed
to
disappear!

Leela became smaller and smaller until it was very hard to find her.

Soon people began to notice she was getting quieter and quieter.

Some days, Leela just sat in her room looking outside. Even the birds didn't make her smile anymore. Leela was lonely and knew she could really use some help.

**Help finally came when Leela had almost given up.
Leela started speaking to her teacher after class.
She helped Leela and her family find a
counselor - someone Leela could trust
and speak to about her feelings.**

Leela visited her counselor every week. Sometimes they drew and sometimes they played with sand. Some days they talked about feelings and some days Leela stayed small and silent.

As the days passed, Leela began to talk about all the things she had tried to forget. She started keeping a journal of her days.

Leela tried hard not to keep her feelings and thoughts inside all the time. She began to speak more at school. As time passed, she even began to make new friends.

As Leela got help, birds chirped and sang their songs. Flowers again opened their brilliant and beautiful petals for Leela. Soft grass caressed her feet. The clouds finally came back with Leela's happy memories of rain.

The sun even spoke to Leela,
"Shine now beautiful Leela.
This is your home now.
You're safe here. You're safe now."

Then came the gushing rain. Oh cool, delicious rain. Mixing with Leela's tears, soothing and comforting her. Now, Leela smiles again as she takes a deep breath of fresh air.

Discussion Questions

The following may be used for exploration and discussion:

❖ Name a time when you had to say goodbye to something or someone you loved. What were some things you felt inside? What helped/helps you with your feelings?

❖ Have you ever gone through something like Leela did? Did you tell anyone what you were going through or get help?

❖ What happens inside your body when you are feeling: 1) sad 2) worried 3) afraid 4) hurt 5) angry? For example, some people get stomach aches when they are worried. Other people have trouble breathing when they are worried.

❖ Who can you go to for help if you need it?

❖ Draw or write about what helps you feel safe. This can include people, things, favorite places, pets, etc.

❖ Find a place in nature that makes you happy or makes you smile. See if you can find something small from this place (a leaf, pine cone, rock, etc.) that can help you remember this place.

Additional Resources

Association for Play Therapy
http://www.a4pt.org

National Child Traumatic Stress Network
http://www.nctsn.org

International Society for the Study of Trauma and Dissociation
http://www.isst-d.org

About the Author

Rita Patel Garcia, LCSW, RYT is a licensed psychotherapist and registered yoga teacher. She specializes in providing a holistic and integrated approach to concerns such as anxiety, depression, self-esteem, trauma, grief and loss, parenting, and relationship struggles. Ms. Patel Garcia works with children, adolescents, and adults.

In addition to her work as a psychotherapist and play therapist, Ms. Patel Garcia teaches yoga for trauma survivors. She is passionate about helping trauma survivors reconnect to and find safety in their bodies. Originally from the Fiji Islands, Ms. Patel Garcia currently lives in Georgia.

For more information: **www.patelgarciacounseling.com** or (404) 319-0053

About the Illustrator

Dr. Angelika Domschke is a scientist and artist devoted to educate, inspire and promote health. As an accomplished artist under the name "Angel" she has exhibited her illustrations, paintings and sculptures internationally in prestigious Galleries such as Galleria Romanelli in Florence, Italy and many locations throughout Switzerland, Germany and the United States.

Dr. Domschke became scientifically involved in the field of children's health when she studied the mechanism of visualization and its effect on the human body and published her children's book *How Nicky Kicks His Cold* (**www.kickthecold.com**). Dr. Domschke works as a research scientist developing advanced polymeric materials for medical applications.

For more information: www.angelikart.com